● **soho**
● theatre company

Soho Theatre Company presents

# MEETING MYSELF COMING BACK

## by **Kerry Hood**

Developed in partnership with Graeae Theatre Company and writernet through the disPlay4 project

First performed at the Soho Theatre on 18 July 2002

**Performances in the Lorenz Auditorium**

Soho Theatre is supported by

  **Bloomberg**

gettyimages

# MEETING MYSELF COMING BACK

by **Kerry Hood**

| | |
|---|---|
| **Mother** | Annie Fitzmaurice |
| **Catherine** | Joanna Holden |
| **Father** | Clive Mendus |
| **Meg** | Lisa Moule |

| | |
|---|---|
| **Director** | John Wright |
| **Designer** | Tom Piper |
| **Lighting Designer** | Jason Taylor |
| **Sound Designer** | John Leonard |
| **Assistant to the Director** | Vicky Jones |

| | |
|---|---|
| **Production Manager** | Nick Ferguson |
| **Stage Manager** | Lorraine Tozer |
| **Deputy Stage Manager** | Charlotte Padgham |
| **Chief Technician** | Nick Blount |
| **Production Electricians** | Sebastian Barraclough |
| | Adrian Peterkin |
| **Scenery built and painted by** | Robert Knight Ltd |
| **Tap Instructor** | Becky Kitter |

Soho Theatre Company would like to thank:
Hannah Bentley
Helen Costley
Rachel Donovan
Graeae
writernet

Press Representation
Angela Dias at Soho Theatre (020 7478 0142)
Advertising
Haymarket Advertising for Guy Chapman Associates
Graphic Design
Jane Harper

Soho Theatre and Writers' Centre
21 Dean Street
London W1D 3NE
Admin: 020 7287 5060
Fax: 020 7287 5061
Box Office: 020 7478 0100
www.sohotheatre.com
email: box@sohotheatre.com

# THE COMPANY

## Cast

### Annie Fitzmaurice Mother

Theatre includes *Shoot Me In the Heart* (Told by An Idiot/The Gate Theatre), *Twelfth Night* (Northern Stage/Newcastle Playhouse); *Animal Farm* (Northern Stage/Young Vic and International Tour); *Tales of Fraulein Pollinger* (Theatre Box); *The Just* (RSC Fringe); *Throwing Stones* (Theatre Upstairs); *Romeo and Juliet* (Nexus); *Daisy Pulls It Off* (Link Theatre) and *Wish Me Luck* (Independent Theatre Company).

Television includes *Holby City*, *A Good Thief*, *Coronation Street*, *Brookside*, *Cerddwn Ymlaen*, *Extremely Dangerous*, *The Bill* and *Body Story*.

Other work includes collaborating on the devised radio sitcom pilot *The Newbury Arms* (BBC Manchester) and two short independent films, *Wightsmith* and *Donna*.

### Joanna Holden Catherine

Most recent work includes *Romeo and Juliet*, *A Ballroom of Romance*, *Play*, *Pinnochio* (Northern Stage Ensemble); *Pondlife* (Bush Theatre); *The Children's Hour* (Royal National Theatre); *The Kitchen* (Royal Court Theatre); *A Servant of Two Masters* (The Sheffield Crucible) and *The Ubu Plays* (Gate Theatre).

### Clive Mendus Father

Theatre includes *The Visit*, *Help I'm Alive*, *The Street of Crocodiles* and *Caucasian Chalk Circle* (Theatre de Complicite); *Much Ado About Nothing* (Royal Exchange, Manchester); *Ay! Carmela!* (Contact Theatre, Manchester); *The Jungle Book* (Young Vic); *Epitaph for the Whales* (Gate Theatre); *India Song* (Theatr Clwyd, Wales); *Arsenic and Old Lace* (Lyceum Theatre, Edinburgh); *A Better Day* (Stratford East, London); *The Faerie Queen* (Queen Elizabeth Hall, London) and *Oedipus Tyrannos* (BAC). Worked with many touring companies including ATC and five productions with the Medieval Players (UK and Australia). As a soloist in *Pygmalion Too* and *The Master of Headland Hall* (UK and Stockholm).

Television includes *Karaoke* (Dennis Potter); *Peter and the Wolf* (Emmy Award winner, Spitting Image); *The Last American Lift Operator, Burning Ambition* (Complicite/BBC); *I Lovett* and *The Chemist*.

As a Director work includes *Mustard Gas and Roses* and *The Treatment* (Catapult Theatre); *The Breeze* (Hoi-Polloi Theatre); *Mon. Henri de Toulouse Lautrec dans son Cabaret* (Third Party); *Kitchen* (Waterfront, Norwich); *Doing Bush* (AK 47 Theatre Company) and for the aerialists Momentary Fusion. Clive has also worked as an Assistant Director and as a teacher at prisons, drama academies, numerous schools and colleges.

**Lisa Moule**  Meg

Lisa trained at Lecoq in Paris and at Melbourne University. Theatre credits include *Newsrevue* (Canal Café); *Richard III*, *Macbeth* (Gasworks, Melbourne); *New Works* (Lamama Theatre, Melbourne) and children's theatre tours.

Film and television includes *Mr. Nice Guy*, *Jackie Chan* and *Shorts* (Melbourne Film Festival).

## Company

**Kerry Hood**  Writer

Plays include *Dancing on Bubble Pack* (1997); *Praise the Lord and Michael Fish; Paj and Pompetry* (a short comedy as part of *Western Front* at Bristol Old Vic/Touring, 1999) and *Feng Shui at Hair by Christine* (Bristol New Vic Basement, 2000). *Meeting Myself Coming Back* (originally named *Eff-Harry-Stow*) was developed with Soho Theatre Company in partnership with Graeae Theatre Company and writernet through the disPlay4 project. Kerry has also written a children's novel *Come Back, Vanishing Boy* and won the Writers' Bureau Short Fiction Competition (2000) for *Space Cadet*.

**Vicky Jones**  Assistant to the Director

Vicky has recently directed a presentation for the Young Writers' Festival at the Royal Court and is currently also a reader for the Festival. She has also been invited to join the Directors' course at the Royal Court. Vicky has directed several productions in London at the Edinburgh Fringe Festival including *Airswimming* and *Broken.*

**John Leonard**  Sound Designer

Most recent productions include *Benefactors* (tour); *The Feast of Snails*, *Private Lives* (West End/Broadway); *Antony and Cleopatra*, *Much Ado About Nothing*, *The Prisoner's Dilemma*, *The Merchant of Venice* (RSC); *Macbeth* (Ludlow Festival); *A Christmas Carol*, *The Winslow Boy* (Chichester Festival Theatre); *Office*, *Kiss Me Like You Mean It* (Soho Theatre Co.); *King Lear* (Theatr Clwyd); *Sweeney Todd* (Wolsey Theatre); *The Importance of Being Earnest* (Chichester Festival Theatre/New York/ Australia); *Madame Tussaud's Exhibition* (New York, Amsterdam); *Little Foxes*, *To The Green Fields and Beyond*, *Orpheus Descending*, *The Real Thing* and *Helpless* (Donmar Warehouse). For Almeida Theatre Company productions include *Lulu* (also in Washington), *King Lear*, *Faith Healer*, *Platonov*, *The Tempest*, *Mr. Peter's Connections*, *Coriolanus*, *Richard II* (also in New York and Japan) *Celebration/The Room* and *Plenty*. John is a director of Aura Sound Design Ltd.

**Tom Piper**  Designer

Theatre designs include: *The Tempest, Henry VI Parts 1, 2 & 3, Richard III, Romeo and Juliet, A Midsummer Night's Dream, Measure for Measure, Bartholomew Fair, The Broken Heart, Spring Awakening, A Patriot for*

*Me, Much Ado About Nothing, Troilus and Cressida, A Month In the Country* and *The Spanish Tragedy* (Royal Shakespeare Company); *The Birthday Party, Blinded by the Sun* (Royal National Theatre); *Denial* (Bristol Old Vic); *Miss Julie* (Haymarket Theatre); *Hedda Gabler* (Plymouth Theatre Royal & No 1 Tour); *Penny for a Song* (Whitehall & UK Tour); *The Spirit of Annie Ross* (The Gate Theatre, Dublin); *Helpless, Frame 312, A Lie of the Mind, The American Imports Season* including *Three Days of Rain* (Donmar Warehouse); *Oh! What a Lovely War* (RNT Mobile Tour); *Scissor Happy* (Duchess Theatre); *Wallace and Gromit – A Grand Night Out* (Peacock Theatre and National Tour); *Kindertransport* (Vaudeville, Watford and Soho Theatre Company); *Four Plays: Four Weeks* (re-opening season at Soho Theatre Company); *The Crucible, Six Characters in Search of an Author* (Abbey Theatre, Dublin); *Backpay, Cockroach, Who?* (Royal Court); *Waking, Tulip Futures, Ripped, My Goat, Rockstation* (Soho Theatre Company); *The Masterbuilder* (Lyceum, Edinburgh); *Endgame, Dumbstruck, Macbeth* (Tron Theatre); *The Price* (York Theatre Royal); *The Way of the World* (Lyric Hammersmith); *The Duchess of Malfi* (Wyndham's, Greenwich and Tour); *Sweet Panic, The Philanderer, Disposing of the Body* (Hampstead Theatre) and *The Cherry Orchard, The Frogs* (Nottingham Playhouse).

Tom has won the London Fringe Best Design Award twice.

## Jason Taylor  Lighting Designer

Current and recent theatre includes *My Night with Reg, Dealer's Choice* (Birmingham Rep); *Oh What A Lovely War, As You Like It, Romeo and Juliet* (Regent's Park Open Air Theatre); *The Mikado, The Yoeman of the Guard, Iolanthe* (D'Oyly Carte at the Savoy); *Single Spies* (Bath and tour); *Abigail's Party* (Bath and Hampstead Theatre) and *Dead Eye Boy* (Hampstead Theatre). Past productions for Soho Theatre Company include: *Behsharam* (co-production with Birmingham Rep), *Office, Kiss Me Like You Mean It, The Coming World, Navy Pier, Angels and Saints, Stop Kiss, Jump, Mr Malinoff, Jump, Be My Baby, Station, Billy and the Crab Lady, Cadillac Ranch,* and *The Jerusalem Syndrome*. Jason was also a Consultant to Soho Theatre Company. Other theatre includes a further eight seasons at the Regent's Park Open Air Theatre and thirty productions at Nottingham Playhouse.

## John Wright  Director

John Wright is a co-founder of Trestle Theatre Company and he directed most of their work including *Top Story, Ties That Bind* and *The Edge*. In 1992 he co-founded his present company, Told By An Idiot with Paul Hunter and Hayley Carmichael. John has directed the majority of their productions. Most recently this includes *Happy Birthday Mr Deka D* (a co-production with Traverse Theatre Company), *I Can't Wake Up* and *Aladdin and his Wonderful Lamp* (co-productions with Lyric, Hammersmith). His other work includes *Hamlet* and *The Changeling* (Third Party Theatre Company in conjunction with BAC). He is currently working on a new opera for Opera Circus and *The Dumb Waiter* by Harold Pinter, in Paris.

## Author's Note

This play is dedicated to my brother Craig Hood (1958–1996).

*Meeting Myself Coming Back* belongs to my family whose skew-whiff vision of the world and its absurdities, tragedies and joys have made me question, challenge and celebrate the feasibility of living outside the loop.

Thank you to: writernet, Graeae and Soho Theatre for recognising my writing voice; to my husband Allan Edwards, without whom I wouldn't live.

# ● soho
## ● theatre company

Situated in the very heart of London's West End, Soho Theatre and Writers' Centre is home to the pioneering Soho Theatre Company. Opening in 2000, the venue was a Lottery success story and quickly established itself as one of London's key producing theatres.

*'a glittering new theatre in Dean Street'* The Times

Soho is passionate in its commitment to new writing, producing a year-round programme of bold, original and accessible new plays – many of them from first-time playwrights.

*'a foundry for new talent... one of the country's leading producers of new writing'* Evening Standard

Soho aims to be the first port of call for the emerging writer. The unique Writers' Centre invites writers at any stage of their career to submit scripts and receives, reads and reports on over 2,000 per year. In addition to the national Verity Bargate Award – a competition aimed at new writers – it runs an extensive series of programmes from the innovative Under 11s Scheme, Young Writers' Group (14–25s) and Westminster Prize (encouraging local writers) to a comprehensive workshop programme and Writers' Attachment Scheme working to develop writers not just in the theatre but also for radio, TV and film.

*'a creative hotbed... not only the making of theatre but the cradle for new screenplay and television scripts'* The Times

Contemporary, comfortable, air-conditioned and accessible, Soho Theatre is busy from early morning to late at night. Alongside the production of new plays, it's also an intimate venue to see leading comedians from the UK and US in an eclectic programme mixing emerging new talent with established names. Soho Theatre is home to Café Lazeez, serving delicious Indian fusion dishes downstairs or upstairs a lively, late bar with a 1am licence.

*'London's coolest theatre by a mile'* Midweek

Soho Theatre Company is developing its work outside the building, producing in Edinburgh and on tour in the UK whilst expanding the scope of its work with writers. It hosts the annual Soho Writers' Festival – now in its third year which brings together innovative practitioners from the creative industries with writers working in theatre, film, TV, radio, literature and poetry. Our programme aims to challenge, entertain and inspire writers and audiences from all backgrounds.

*'scorching debut brings Festival to life'* Daily Telegraph on Shan Khan's **Office** which opened the 2001 Edinburgh International Festival.

## ● **soho**
● theatre company

**Soho Theatre and Writers' Centre**
21 Dean Street, London W1D 3NE
Admin: 020 7287 5060 Fax: 020 7287 5061
Box Office: 020 7478 0100 Minicom: 020 7478 0136
www.sohotheatre.com      email: box@sohotheatre.com

*Gordon's.*

**Bars and Restaurant**
Café Lazeez brasserie serves Indian-fusion dishes until 12pm. Late bar open until 1am. The Gordon's Terrace serves Gordons* and Tonic and range of soft drinks and wine.

**Email information list**
For free regular programme updates and offers, join our free email information list by emailing box@sohotheatre.com

**Hiring the theatre**
Soho Theatre has a range of rooms and spaces for hire. Please contact the theatre managers on 020 7287 5060 or email hires@sohotheatre.com for further details.

## Soho Theatre Company

## THE SOHO THEATRE DEVELOPMENT CAMPAIGN

Soho Theatre Company receives core funding from Westminster City Council and London Arts. However, in order to provide as diverse a programme as possible and expand our audience development and outreach work, we rely upon additional support. Many projects are only made possible by donations from trusts, foundations, individuals and corporate involvement.

All our major sponsors share a common commitment to developing new areas of activity with the arts and with the assistance of Arts and Business New Partners, encouraging a creative partnership with the sponsors and their employees. This translates into special ticket offers, creative writing workshops, innovative PR campaigns and hospitality events.

Our **Studio Seats** campaign is to raise money and support for the vital and unique work that goes on behind the scenes at Soho Theatre. Alongside reading and assessing over 2000 scripts a year, we also work intensively with writers through workshops, showcases, writers' discussion nights and rehearsed readings. For only £300 you can take a seat in the Education and Development Studio to support this crucial work.

If you would like to help, or have any questions, please contact the development department on 020 7287 5060 or at development@sohotheatre.com or visit our website www.sohotheatre.com/dev

We are immensely grateful to all of our sponsors and donors for their support and commitment.

**Research & Development:** Calouste Gulbenkian Foundation • Samuel Goldwyn Foundation • Harold Hyam Wingate Foundation • Spring Quiz Teams **Education:** Anon • Delfont Foundation • Hyde Park Place Estate Charity • International Asset Management • Madeleine Hamel • John Lyon's Charity • Mathilda and Terence Kennedy Charitable Trust • Royal Victoria Hall Foundation • The St James's Trust • Shaftesbury PLC • The Kobler Trust • The Pitt Street Foundation **Building:** The Rose Foundation **Access:** Bridge House Estates Trust
**Individuals: Gold Patrons:** Anon • Katie Bradford • Julie & Robert Breckman • David Day • Raphael Djanogly • Jack and Linda Keenan **Silver Patrons:** Anon • Rob Brooks **Bronze Patrons:** Samuel French Ltd • Solid Management • Paul & Pat Zatz **Studio Seats:** Anon • Jo Apted • Peter Backhouse • Leslie Bolsom • Mrs Alan Campbell-Johnson • David Day • Raphael Djanogly • Imtiaz and Susan Dossa • Anthony Gardner • Catherine Graham-Harrison and Nicholas Warren • Sally A Graudons • Hope Hardcastle • Bruce Hyman • Roger Jospé • Jeremy Levison • John and Jean McCaig • Annie Parker • Eric and Michéle Senat • Simonetta Valentini • Marc Vlessing

**SOHO THEATRE and WRITERS' CENTRE**
In 1996, Soho Theatre Company was awarded an £8 million Lottery grant from the Arts Council of England to help create the Soho Theatre + Writers' Centre. An additional £2.6 million in matching funds was raised and over 500 donors supported the capital appeal. The full list of supporters is displayed on our website at www.sohotheatre.com/thanks.htm

**BUILDING SUPPORTERS**
Supported by the Arts Council of England with National Lottery funds

The Lorenz Auditorium supported by Carol and Alan Lorenz
**Principal sponsor:** Getty Images
**Rooms:** Gordon's Terrace supported by Gordon's Gin • The Education and Development Studio supported by the Foundation for Sport and the Arts • Equity Trust Fund Green Room • The Vicky Arenson Writers' Seminar Room • Writers' Room supported by The Samuel Goldwyn Foundation • Unity Theatre Writers' Room • Writers' Room supported by Nick Hornby and Annette Lynton Mason • The Marchpole Dressing Room • Wardrobe supported by Angels the Costumiers • The Peter Sontar Production Office • The White Light Control Room • The Strand Dimmer Room • The Dennis Selinger Meeting Room
**Building:** Simon Catt Berger Oliver • Derick and Margaret Coe • The Esmée Fairbairn Foundation • The Rose Foundation • The Meckler Foundation • Roberta Sacks
**Soho first:** BAFTA • Cowboy Films Ltd • Simons Muirhead & Burton
**Gold patrons:** Eric Abraham • Jill and Michael Barrington • Roger Bramble • Anthony and Elizabeth Bunker • John Caird • David and Pat Chipping • John Cohen at Clintons • Nadia and Mark Crandall • David Day • Michael and Maureen Edwards • Charles Hart • Hat Trick Productions • David Huyton at Moore Stephens • Miriam and Norman Hyams • David Jackson at Pilcher Hershman • The St James' Trust • John Kelly–European Quality • Mr and Mrs Philip Kingsley • The McKenna Charitable Trust • Nancy Meckler and David Aukin • Michael and Mimi Naughton • Robert Ogden CBE • Diana Quick • Christian Roberts • Lyn Schlesinger • Peter M Schlesinger • Carl Teper • Diana and Richard Toeman • Richard Wilson OBE • Margaret Wolfson

**GRAEae**
THEATRE COMPANY

Established in 1980 by Nabil Shaban and Richard Tomlinson, Graeae is Britain's leading theatre company of people with physical and sensory impairments.

Funded by the Arts Council of England, London Arts and the Association of London Government, and led since 1997 by Artistic Director Jenny Sealey, Graeae tours nationally twice a year and occasionally internationally, with imaginative and exciting productions of both classic and newly-commissioned theatre.

Graeae's aim is to redress the exclusion of people with physical and sensory impairments from performance and is concerned with developing high quality, genuinely pioneering theatre in both its aesthetic and content.

As well as touring, the company has a strong commitment to training disabled people in performance and other production skills, young peoples' theatre, outreach and education.

"It is quite a performance...a striking and cleverly-judged production by Jenny Sealey... This is a major piece of theatre from a company that refuses to be relegated to the sidelines, and it is acted with honesty and terrific chutzpah..." **** *The Guardian, on 'peeling', 6 April 2002, Soho Theatre*

Interchange Studios
213 Haverstock Hill
London
NW3 4QP
T 020 7681 4755
F 020 7681 4756
M 020 7681 4757
info@graeae.org
www.graeae.org

writernet has evolved from New Playwrights Trust. NPT was established in 1985, as a 'grassroots' public service body targeting primarily those writers entering the playwriting profession. writernet now works with new writing in all performance contexts. More established writers are also now benefiting from our work. writernet provides writers for all forms of live and recorded performance – working at any stage in their career – with a range of services which enable them to pursue their careers more effectively. By helping writers negotiate their way through the industry from all parts of the country and a wide diversity of backgrounds, we aim to enable the realisation of potential – often from connections not accessible via established channels. Through training we encourage innovation, both through our commitment to a diversity of voices and our ability to stay abreast of trends in thinking and practice outside the new writing mainstream.

## disPlay4

A pioneering cross media development programme, disPlay4 provided theatre writing apprenticeships with a professional theatre company for four disabled experienced writers, with additional access to training and placement in radio and television. Four writers, Kerry Hood, Danny Start, Jamie Beddard and Angela McNab, worked with dramaturg Kaite O'Reilly for a whole year, gaining access to workshops, masterclasses, productions, production and script meetings, and an opportunity to immerse themselves within, and learn about, the workings of a theatre company which produces new writing. The development process culminated with a showing of their work in progress as part of Soho Theatre's Writers' Festival in November 2001.

disPlay4 was a partnership between writernet, Soho Theatre Company and Graeae, and is supported by the Arts Council of England and the Belvedere Trust.

First published in 2002 by Oberon Books Ltd.
(incorporating Absolute Classics)
521 Caledonian Road, London N7 9RH
Tel: 020 7607 3637 / Fax: 020 7607 3629

e-mail: oberon.books@btinternet.com
www.oberonbooks.com

A catalogue record for this book is available from the British Library.

ISBN: 1 84002 335 X

Cover photo: James Cotier/Getty Images/Stone

Printed in Great Britain by Antony Rowe Ltd, Chippenham.

*I'm waiting to speak to this home, to speak. An extraordinary speech.*

*But it won't come…*

# Characters

CATHERINE
aged twenty-one

FATHER
aged forty-three

MOTHER
aged thirty-three

MEG
sister, aged ten/eleven

# ACT ONE

## Scene 1

*1 May 2000. 3 pm. Doorstep, 21 Pontellier Avenue. House For Sale sign.*

*Sound: sea, distant.*

*CATHERINE is frozen with fear; one hand holds front door key, one clutches a Safeway bag. She sees MOTHER (unseen to us) in kitchen, FATHER (unseen to us) waiting stiffly on the stairs. She closes eyes…*

*Blackout. Lights up…*

*…opens; rubs head; mouths silent mantras: 'Buy One Get One Free Buy One Get One Free thank you thank you thank you.' Shifts weight, in pain. Struggles with key.*

*Fade to black.*

## Scene 2

*Same day, 3:05 pm. Hallway, Pontellier Avenue.*

*Wipe-board: 'Daedalus, Marcel & Woolf Thank You For Viewing."*

*CATHERINE is frozen. Silence…*

CATHERINE: (*To audience.*) This has been a week of words. Two in particular have stood out: 'Vestibule' and 'Bamboozle'. The first is where I am now; the second has an hour-long history and I'm saving it, like a bit of birthday cake.

*She looks to stairs then to kitchen: MOTHER's territory. CATHERINE automatically goes to step towards it/her…then remembers the last time she was there. Gasps.*

*Sound: house alarm.*

*She fumbles in bag for alarm code. Now she sees (we do not) in her peripheral vision FATHER waiting behind her, by front door. Alarm box is by her head (she doesn't need to walk). She fumbles/switches it off.*

I could be a burglar or a time-waster or a liar but the estate agents never asked. Even if they had, I couldn't… (*Puts fingers to mouth.*) A week of words. And it is only Monday – (*Anxiously.*) – 'Mid-afternoon with Mal and Minty' time probably – don't know I don't know I know it is Monday May Day my watch has gone. Locked up, safe. Still in hospital, safe. I should be there still, safe. But I nearly had an operation today. Nearly Bamboozled. (*Rubs head.*)

*Lights gradually up…on Flashback Area.*

I'm going to my flat-house – (*Rubs head; looks to Flashback Area.*) – in here. Show you my timetable, safe. Start with Thursdays – flat-house to The Safe Way, Fridays – Post Office, Saturdays – I'm telling you so it won't be a shock when it's happening…

*Flashback Area: fade.*

…only this week is being disobedient. I see more. Been pushing today away but it's come, it's come. (*Urgently.*) Let's go home. (*Closes eyes.*)

*Blackout.*

# Scene 3

*Four days earlier: Thursday, 7 am. Flashback Area: CATHERINE's flat.*

*She is kneeling, cutting out magazine recipes.*

CATHERINE: (*Earnestly.*) On Thursdays I go through The Safe Way magazine. If you have a loyalty card, it's free. I mostly just get the magazine with it. I don't think that makes me very loyal. I cut out each recipe and its picture called a Fig Dot. The Fig Dot is ladies' hands, unless it is half-term when The Safe Way teaches young people how to recognise a kitchen. Then the Fig Dots are children's entire faces –

This Fig Dot and the words disagree: the boy has a flash of flour across his nose but flour isn't even mentioned. Fig Three: he is smiling. At a wooden spoon. It looks dangerous.

(*Points at next Fig.*) Mixing bowl, chocolate, cereal. He's doing this (*Tongue out in concentration.*) to make sure each paper saucer has thirty-seven Rice Krispies.

The recipes start with own-label ingredients e.g. for Spaghetti Bolognaise: The Safe Way Chopped Tomatoes…but you can use another brand or a tin of unchopped gulpy tomatoes. It isn't very loyal but the spaghetti bolognaise doesn't know because it is food and doesn't have feelings of moral responsibility.

(*Stroking chair.*) Mug-of-tea stain. This sleeve hides it, like French queens with tall wigs over their nits. If the chair was a lady, her visiting friends would never know. It isn't a lady. It doesn't have visitors. I would remember a chair ringing the doorbell.

(*Tries to stand.*) I shouldn't do it but I do it every Thursday because I do it every Thursday. (*Has to sit.*)

There is a question on form DLA2, in bold in case you don't understand, like people shouting if you're deaf. *Do You Stumble How Often Do You Stumble Do You Stumble When You Are On Your Own Do You Fall How Often Do You Fall Do You Fall When You Are On Your Own.* Six questions pretending to be one. There are no question marks, which is a punctuation error unless the form wants a certain answer. DLA stands for Living Allowance. The D is for another word. You don't have to say it you don't have to put your hand up and say the word.

*Blackout.*

# Scene 4

*1 May 2000. 3:10 pm. Hallway, Pontellier Avenue, as at end of Scene 2. MOTHER (unseen) in kitchen, baking. FATHER in blackout behind her by front door.*

CATHERINE: (*Anxiously, only eyes moving.*) Monday today May Day. After the nearly-operation, I got these keys from Mr, Mr and Mr Estate Agents. *I* got them. *I* pointed to this photo. They were Bank Holiday-busy. They didn't look at me – it should only happen in a book. They *gave* the keys to me. To twenty-one Pontellier Avenue.

*FATHER gradually lit. CATHERINE feels his presence. Looks to Flashback Area.*

(*Fearfully.*) Let's do Thursdays again.

*Blackout.*

# Scene 5

*Four days earlier: Thursday, 8 am. Flashback Area: Safeway.*

*CATHERINE holds a purse and Safeway bag.*

CATHERINE: When I've cut out each recipe and the Fig Dot it is nearly seven-thirty am.

(*Holding up bag.*) I come here. The Safe Way is straight. The aisles are straight, checkouts in rows, straight. The Safe Way is also in America. Same uniform but not tights – panty hose. They don't queue – they wait in line. It is still waiting, whichever side of the Atlantic.

I come like this (*Head down.*) to the faggots. I don't like faggots. I like the aisle. It is cool and most of the time my head is hot. There is a lot in my head. I need my list like horse blinkers so there won't be too many words here. (*Rubs head.*) I am used to not allowing them out, but they still run around inside, with only my lips (*Mouthing.*) moving, outside.

(*Looks at list; lips move.*) This is me. And what I can't do once I have left my head.

(*Self-consciously looks peripherally. Whispers.*) The security guard has entirely no hair. And thick short arms that go out, in, out like a string of sausages. He lets you take food for nothing. Usually this is called stealing. The Safe Way calls it Buy One Get One Free. You could keep buying one getting one free, never be without one to look at, to hold, a flash blink newness of it every time you open your cupboard. My mother sent me to school with a tinned tuna roll then…

*Beat.*

…goes in the cupboard for her secret tin of smiles with a different label over it.

I shouldn't need to keep buying tuna. I'm entirely twenty-one. My father would say (*As FATHER.*) one is never too young for harsh facts too old for discipline it makes one British damn well counts. (*Matter-of-fact.*) My father would say that but he's dead.

*Silence.*

I apologise for the lack of drama, the lack of bigthingness.

(*Aware of security guard, she stacks/unstacks tuna.*) Do You Speak How Often Do You Speak Do You Speak When You Are On Your Own Do You Speak How Often Do You Speak Do You Speak.

*Fade to black.*

# Scene 6

*1 May 2000. 3:15 pm. Hallway, Pontellier Avenue.*

*CATHERINE is adding to wipe-board: 'Thank you for shopping at The Safe Way'.*

*Sound: food processor in kitchen.*

*CATHERINE turns. MOTHER appears at kitchen door. CATHERINE moves one step to her…but we see a flash/shadow of FATHER as he crosses between them and enters lounge…to black. MOTHER…to black.*

*Lights gradually up on Flashback Area as…*

CATHERINE: Show you my Friday timetable. What I do every – what I did *this* Friday.

*Blackout.*

# Scene 7

*Three days earlier: Friday, 9 am. Flashback Area: Post Office.*

*Sound: intermittent 'Cashier number one please' etc.*

*CATHERINE queues, bag at her feet. Reads competition entry form. During scene, she indicates moving queue by picking up/putting down bag.*

CATHERINE: Qantas doesn't have a 'u'. It is right, it's just that you expect 'u' to follow the 'q'. If you're English. (*Shifts weight; looks around person in front.*) Words have silent parts to them…

*Person in queue turns. CATHERINE looks down.*

…like looks.

(*Holding up competition form.*) Competition tie-breakers have to convince the reader you deserve to win. You write the entire world of the prize in twenty-five words.

Millions of words in it, the world. You could pretend it's
1941 and you are only allowed two ounces a week. But
this is the next century and you can have as many as you
can say at other people. You can't say every word in one
lifetime, unless you become an acronym factory and
scrunch words like 'Qantas'. I say two a day, which is
plenty for me.

If I win, I go to Australia. There isn't anyone I need to
tell. I live on my own entirely.

(*Looks at shelves.*) Silver keys for grandmas to put on
sponge cakes. I had a sponge three years ago when I was
eighteen. Grandmas didn't make it. It was trapped in a
bag from The Safe Way. It tasted of the bag. It didn't
have a key. I belonged to the Government from thirteen
to eighteen.

*Beat.*

I nearly had a cake for my thirteenth –

(*Deflects by memorising shelves.*) Bubble-blowers, doll's
dummies… If I had a dummy, I don't remember.
(*Matter-of-fact.*) I would ask my mother but she's dead.

(*Aware of a face behind; holds breath…exhales.*) It is only a
lady. You shouldn't stop breathing if you want to live.

(*Deflects by looking up and reading sign.*) 'We Need You:
Fostering is a Job for Life'. I had fosterers when I was
thirteen. They got bored waiting for my words. Gave me
to the Government, to a Home for Children and Young
People, where a five-year timetable is ticked off for you.
Where Children and Young People played ping-pong,
with me on a chair, watching.

(*Takes out pink DLA withdrawal slip.*) DLA is money you
get for answering questions on obstacles to your physical
and or mental happiness. I get the low rate because of

the box about how what I am affects my happiness. There is no box asking who I am but they are not trick questions and there is no tie-breaker. That would discriminate on the grounds of literary incompetence. If you make an error, you paint it with Tippex, photocopy the page, start as if what's underneath was never underneath. But if you look closely you can see little bits of past answers, which makes your eyes hurt. So you don't look.

I filled in the DLA form at the Home, same day I cut my hair off with nail scissors. The Adults: (*Patronisingly, as ADULT.*) It is a cry for help. I thought it was because I wanted to lengthen my steroidy face.

*CATHERINE rocks side to side.*

(*As ADULT.*) Stand still!

It isn't their fault. You don't expect a person to have non-stop hurting hips and if that person can't even say please may I sit down thank you…

I thought about it the same way I am talking now, without quotation marks. You need them on the page…

*Beat.*

…but since my thirteenth birthday I only use speech inside so I don't know the rules. I manage the same two outside words a day – (*Mouths 'Thank you'.*) No one at the Home asked about my father or my mother.

(*Looks up at man in front.*) He is doing Lom Pom singing, for his own self. His parcel might have something on the… (*Looks down, avoiding eye contact.*) …list of dangerous post, (*Indicates list on wall.*) things you can't send e.g. filth you can't send filth doesn't say what type.

(*Sings from 'Carmen', copying man, her eyes anxiously following him and CCTV.*) Pom Lom Pompom, Pom Pom Lom Pom – infectious materials, you can't send those –

Stop Lom Pomming! The camera sees everything, plays it back, reminds you what you did wrong every second of your life!

(*Deflects by looking up and reading sign.*) 'The Customer Charter: Available in Arabic, Bengali, Chinese, Gujarati, Punjabi, Somali, Urdu and Vietnamese'. (*Following / avoiding CCTV. Excited, afraid.*) I might get a Vietnamese one because in the dictionary of places it looks a beautiful country despite the ravages of war… Nearly in it! Nearly caught on camera in public by Big Brother! I have a Little Sister sharp items must be wrapped or tragedies occur. (*She jerks; head down.*) He is laughing with the cashier – smiling is bad enough creases your eyes but laughing splits your eyebrow I don't do it ever it isn't loyal.

(*Looks up; reads sign. Calms.*) 'Benefit Fraud Hotline Shop Your Neighbour Details Here In Braille.' Mr Braille allows you to communicate without dangerous noises coming out. You can read the world with important things already raised…but if you are blind you don't know about the Hotline! It is an irony or paradox. They are similar and in an ideal world, a human would explain it, how we know a word by its difference from another.

(*Rubbing palm into head.*) I'm putting the Hotline number in the numbers part of my head. You can phone and shop yourself if you don't think you are DLA enough. After paying for being dead, my father left one hundred and six thousand pounds each for my sister and me – which you'll find funny when you know my sister. I have a flat-house and rainy-day account I am grateful for the DLA thank you I need it I hate it.

(*Pushes slip under glass; looks at clock.*) Twelve minutes behind. Bendy line of eyes, on me queue of eyes, on me. Concentrate. List: living creatures, dry ice…

(*Trying to hear cashier through the glass.*) List: words in a straight line that don't make you leave the queue to pick them up.

(*Stares at cashier; shifts weight in time to memorised list.*) Aerosol, asbestos, bomb, clinical waste, corrosive, counterfeit currency, dry ice, filth – all in order, the lady can see – medicine, poison, rat, sharp item, tuna.

(*Takes money. Aloud, to cashier.*) Thank you. (*To audience.*) Two words, plenty.

(*Reads form.*) If I were a Qantas passenger I would dot dot dot: give my legs two seats the entire way to Australia – smallest continent, capital Canberra, chief product wheat – so they could be stroked, by my mother.

*Crosses fingers, then self-consciously passes the queue. Huge moment – we see her walk: a rolling, painful yet hurried and exposed gait.*

*Fade to black.*

# Scene 8

*1 May 2000. 3:20 pm. Hallway, Pontellier Avenue.*

*CATHERINE is adding to wipe-board: 'DLA: Proof of Identity Required Thank You.'*

*She stands fearfully at lounge door. Reads estate agent's blurb.*

CATHERINE: 'Through-lounge: featuring antique MDF cherubs…'

(*Opens purse: door key on a string pinned in purse.*) I did lock my flat-house? Should I go back? Does my flat-house exist when I am not in it? Does it sit nicely?

Or raise its roof and dance backwards to Michael
Jackson?

*MOTHER walks from kitchen into lounge. CATHERINE,
tantalising near, is transfixed by MOTHER during...*

Do I exist – I mean, could I exist, if suddenly I was able
to walk without looking like a metronome? Or am
I entirely hurting hips and dead parents? Could I? Am I?
It's to do with philosophy and will be in the big library.

(*Walks automatically into lounge. To MOTHER.*) Am
I entirely twenty-one yet? (*To audience.*) Born at evening
dinnertime. I have no watch.

'Daedalus, Marcel & Woolf recommend you begin your
tour of Twenty-one Pontellier Avenue along the vestibule
where the viewer will find the kitchen self-explanatory.'

*Looks to kitchen. Blackout. Lights up.*

Rather stop here thank you, in the through-lounge with
its 'ironic use of the dado rail.'

No books. *I* have two hundred and forty-eight – seven.
(*Rubbing head, shifting weight.*) This week I had to go to
the library yesterday not today Monday which is when
I usually go but a) it is May Day b) I had to go to
hospital today but yesterday was Sunday and my little
library is closed on Sundays... (*Calming.*) It used to be
my little chapel. Now they keep rare books up there.
(*Looks up.*) Precious eggs in a nest.

(*Shows two lists.*) Books to take back, books to take from.
So I don't look unblinkered at every published thing, so
I can get home before the world is entirely awake,
staring. Today: Vietnam... Sir Donald Sinden and...six
others. There's a new one on the Princess. She is on the
cover smiling, clinging to her sons. She smiled too
much. No wonder someone didn't like it and killed her.

Every week I have two lists, but one thing leads…like a thesaurus. (*Excited.*) Just finished a book with one hundred thousand words about words. Said *we* make the sign that puts an own-label on a word. We make its meaning because of how it looks, its entire difference from another word. For example, Death… Life.

*There is no discernible difference. Silence.*

That is the theory. How one word works with another. How a person is given a meaning because of how their hip looks when it doesn't work with the other.

Yesterday, Sunday: the *big* library along the coast road, part of Dorset University but open every day to The Community.

*Blackout.*

# Scene 9

*Day earlier: Sunday, 10 am. Flashback Area: Dorset University Library.*

*Sound: Automatic sliding library doors.*

CATHERINE: Turnstiles… How do I get in the words? That lady! She goes to my little library.

(*She watches/copies coughing lady; takes unused library swipe card. Mimics.*) Fed up with this bloody cough…up half the night.

(*She coughs; swipes card; pushes over turnstile. She is in awe.*) You don't have to open your mouth! It knows who you are, doesn't need fingerprints. Some of mine aren't there because I tried to open a red-hot car when I was twelve.

No books, just computers…and Sunday students! With zebra print phones and me in it, their world, looking for the…*itness*, the precious eggs, the code.

(*She stares at students; mimics their stance. Shifts weight rhythmically.*) Please where are the books show me please the books the books the books...

*She hits head; repeats until she is inaudible and we see what 'normal' people see.*

(*Audibly.*) Purple file! Shiny-alive book! I aspire to the file, the precious egg!

(*Sneaking file/book into bag. Eyes fixed on student.*) It is her file, her book. She's laughing, walking entirely like – me! I aspire to *her.* She is the *middle.* Could be my sister couldn't be my sister because a) my sister is younger b) doesn't have hurting hips c) is dead. Accident aged eleven, year before my mother my father –

Playground! The student is every playground every sniggery corner I'm scratched in sent to Coventry in. (*Urgent whisper.*) Disappear walk scurry look away disappear... (*She pushes turnstile...*)

*Sound: turnstile beep.*

(*...and tries to swipe card; nowhere to put it.*) The code the code what's the code? (*Coughing.*) Fed up with this bloody cough. (*Pushes bar; it beeps louder...*)

(*To turnstile.*) Discuss dot dot dot in my opinion dot dot dot in conclusion –

(*As SECURITY.*) Stand aside love give me the book and the bag come on now.

*She is taken by the arm; realises book is alarmed; walks in circles.*

(*As SECURITY.*) Oh (*To onlookers.*) ...how the hell was I to know she i'n't normal?

*Stop beeps. CATHERINE stops. Faces front.*

*Blackout.*

# Scene 10

*1 May 2000. 3:25 pm. Hallway, Pontellier Avenue.*

*CATHERINE is adding to wipe-board: 'Thank You For Maintaining Silence.'*

CATHERINE: Outside my flat-house is a communal garden. I buried my two hundred and forty-eighth book to see if it would grow into a tree of knowledge. It isn't going to happen.

My flat-house is joined to identical ones. On Mondays Mrs Home Care comes for my washing. I manage a thank you. She says (*As Mrs Home Care.*) Don't thank me I'm only doing this because of sodding negative equity.

I wash the pants myself. They have blood on them two weeks out of four. And you don't want to wash someone's pants. Especially if you're behind with the mortgage.

Dougless McAngus looks after the garden. He is Welsh. He always pinches my cheek dirty nails pinching my cheek asks if I mind I do mind don't know how to stop him.

*Pause.*

I didn't want anyone to think I was funny burying the book. So I did it at two am. With an anonymous bin liner over my head.

You'd think you'd be used to laughy people, day in day out. But it's my birthday.

(*Enters lounge.*) Monday May Day. (*Looks at clock.*) Three twenty-five. (*Confused.*) My watch is gone. It won't come here because it is a watch and doesn't have legs, only hands. I left it in hospital, walked away because of being Bamboozled on my big birthday.

This was two rooms: dining-room…lounge, where my mother raised the roof and danced backwards. This was my home.

*Upstage: 1989. Music: Michael Jackson's 'Dirty Diana'.*

*FATHER, MOTHER, MEG (nine) and (imagined) CATHERINE (ten) sit at the table, playing Card Scrabble, making up the words, laughing. FATHER endures music for MOTHER's sake. Throughout, MEG is restless.*

(*Covering smile.*) I'm ten.

*She supplies childhood dialogue/action from downstage position while family mime interaction with her young self.*

There is such a word! 'Yaroops'. (*To MOTHER.*) When Father chases us up the garden – 'ya-roops!' Y-A-R-O-O-P-S.

*MOTHER smiles at FATHER who shakes head in mock despair. MEG drops cards. No one notices. She does it again. Only FATHER notices. They look at each other, challengingly. FATHER chooses to ignore her. Fade scene.*

*Lights up: year later, 1990. Music: Michael Jackson's 'Leave Me Alone'.*

*Card Scrabble, days after MOTHER has miscarried.*

I'm eleven.

*It is MOTHER's turn. FATHER gently puts a hand on her arm to prompt her. She shows no reaction. MEG looks to (imagined) CATHERINE, concerned at MOTHER's mood. FATHER looks helpless but smiles to children. MEG puts down 'Cyprus'. CATHERINE jumps in.*

(*To FATHER.*) Cyprus is a proper word, Father. Where we're going on a proper holiday.

*Cut music. Fade MEG.*

*Year later, 1991. Card Scrabble.*

(*To audience.*) Twelve, nearly thirteen.

*MOTHER puts down a word. FATHER refers to dictionary; stares until she removes word. CATHERINE closes eyes. Fade FATHER and MOTHER. CATHERINE opens eyes.*

She needed to keep the peace, the family in one piece.

*Switches on TV. Sound down.*

'Mid-Afternoon With Mal And Minty.' Mal is telling me not to go away… Minty is telling me what will happen after the break so it won't be a shock… (*As MAL.*) packed May Day programme, Minty (*As MINTY.*) …and the tart tatin sounds delish, Mal, but'll go straight to my hips.

(*As MINTY, smiles to MAL, who smiles front.*) Freemans Catalogue, selling a man in a cagoule, two children in a tent and a lady frying eggs in a field. They are smiling. To show how happy a tent makes you.

*Upstage: FATHER and MOTHER face front. Expressionless.*

(*Recites advert to block parents.*) Diana Princess of Wales fine porcelain doll actual size eighteen inches see for yourself the Catherine Walker gown with matching sequinned bolero the lifelike cornflower blue eyes so tragically snuffed…

*Fade FATHER and MOTHER; CATHERINE relieved but doesn't miss a beat.*

…but now we can all own eighteen inches of her and bend her legs to sit on our TVs delivered in her own box for ninety-nine ninety-nine order within seven days and we will send you free yes free a matching seventeen-inch Dodi Prince of Harrods.

*Music: Michael Jackson's 'Dirty Diana'.*

*Upstage during next speech: 1989 MEG under dining-table plays hide and seek. Calls 'Cathy! Cathy-Cath!' makes ghost noises; giggles. MOTHER reaches under and grabs MEG's leg. They giggle, tickle etc.*

My sister Margaret. I am Catherine because my mother was reading Emily Brontë and I kicked inside when Cathy ran wild on the moors. She had given up reading by the time my sister came. My mother is Diana from Yorkshire. Laughy silly dancey-backwards. My father, Clement. He named my sister in celebration of Thatcherian times. Mother and I call her Meg.

*Music: Michael Jackson's 'Leave Me Alone'.*

*Hide and seek, 1990: MEG under table but MOTHER, days after miscarriage, can't play. FATHER tries but can't become a child. MEG laughs at his attempts. FATHER's childhood/army experiences of being laughed at are barely contained.*

*Cut music. Fade MEG.*

*1991: downstage, adult CATHERINE observes as though for first time.*

(*To FATHER.*) *I'm* here. (*To MOTHER.*) *I'm* still here, *I'll* play.

*MOTHER walks past CATHERINE...making a wide berth around FATHER...to retreat of kitchen...to black.*

(*At TV.*) There's a picture of what's coming up. Mal reads the first thing, Minty the second... You wait for the first thing...but they don't get to it. They are happy waiting.

*MOTHER, tying an apron, appears at kitchen door. FATHER appears at lounge door. Mother shrinks into kitchen...to black. FATHER looks downstage, directly at CATHERINE.*

Minty is waiting to start, I'm waiting to finish. To speak to this home, to speak. (*Opens, closes mouth.*) An extraordinary speech full of bigthingness but it won't come because a) I don't know what it is and b) (*Touches lips.*) but don't go away...

*FATHER steps towards her.*

(*Rushed, afraid.*)…because there's plenty still to come.

*Blackout.*

# Scene 11

*Same day, 3:30 pm. Hallway, Pontellier Avenue.*

*CATHERINE is adding to wipe-board: 'Thank You For Watching'. Between 'For' and 'Watching', she adds 'Not'.*

*MOTHER (unseen) in kitchen. FATHER (unseen) on his way home from work.*

*CATHERINE enters lounge. Looks out of window.*

CATHERINE: If this was my flat-house there'd be the church…and next door, the Dorset South Centre for Community Learning where you can learn to love Jesus or line-dancing. People with special needs go. They have an inability to see or hear or talk or walk or all of those connecting things. Normal people go. They have an inability to put flowers in a vase or go up a single step to music. They watch the special people and say (*FIRST VOICE.*) there but for the grace of God go I (*SECOND VOICE.*) yes fancy being deaf dumb blind limpy how awful bless I'd shoot myself.

I go over. Stand outside Room CFTT – Computing For The Terrified. Watch the Terrifieds get their own disk, password, memory, press 'Enter'…in it, the world!

On Saturdays, I clean the community centre lounge where elderly people go for the day to spill things. I could get paid. The Government is positive about me. It is on the form: 'Positive About' and a drawing of two people. (*Makes two ticks.*) It is an own-label. I don't want to be two ticks so I am a *volunteer* cleaner.

*Walks towards Flashback Area; gaining confidence with safety of imaginative life…*

It's useful having a head that can visit places your legs can't. You can go along your years, make a meaning then not go again. You can be at the Centre in two ticks.

*Blackout.*

# Scene 12

*Two days earlier: Saturday, 8 am. Flashback Area: Community Centre.*

CATHERINE: Saturdays: Mrs Cowfman relies on me. I am here to clean but…the office has files to be filed in filing drawers. Mrs Cowfman has never mentioned my filing. Perhaps she is afraid, perhaps on Mondays she looks at the empty in-tray and her eyes go all wide thinking about a supernatural force in her drawers.

*Sound: buzzer.*

That's my elevenses, which I have at half-past ten. The cook is called Raymond Cook which is a happy coincidence. I get the real elevenses ready: ten tea bags… Marryon bursts in, touches the urn… (*As MARRYON.*) Buggering hell. Marryon is (*Indicates badge.*) Here To Help. Marryon calls me a buggering spastic.

(*Pushes trolley. Shakes tin.*) I buy broken biscuits – it doesn't hurt them, it isn't like bones. Mrs Cowfman says (*As MRS COWFMAN.*) You're a fool to yourself dear the units shan't remember having a biscuit they're losing their minds but if you want to be a philanthropist, well…

Losing their minds. The brain is a room. The mind chooses the wallpaper. And knows it gets a Saturday biscuit. I watch listen disappear like sugar in their tea.

Mr Franx: talking about the Queen to my biscuit tin lid. Marryon takes it.

(*As MARRYON.*) It's not the buggering Queen it's Lady Di.

(*As MR FRANX.*) Lady Di's bringing the monarchy to its knees I can see right through her she has nothing in her but hats.

(*As MARRYON.*) Mr Whatever-your-buggering-name-is you are a buggering old idiot how many times: Lady Di is BUGGERING DEAD.

You can't see right through a being. There are muscles in the way, bones. Bones keep you attached. My mother's were like broken biscuits before she was buried.

*Fade to black.*

# Scene 13

*1 May 2000. 3:35 pm. Hallway, Pontellier Avenue.*

*Sound: phone ringing.*

*CATHERINE reads agent's blurb; looks to kitchen for MOTHER, then to phone. She picks up the receiver; opens mouth –*

*FATHER, with briefcase, enters front door. CATHERINE jumps, shakes head to caller; puts down phone. FATHER walks into kitchen…to black.*

CATHERINE: My father worked for BT 'in communications'. When he had had a bad day he came home and communicated it to my mother. Ever since I was eleven, Meg ten. Since the holiday, where he showed us his army days. Cyprus.

*CATHERINE observes and joins in with the action from downstage as her family mime interaction with her young self.*

*Upstage: Moving car, Cyprus 1990. MOTHER and MEG laugh. FATHER tries not to laugh.*

Driving through Episkopi Bay: father says (*As FATHER.*) this road belongs to Queen Elizabeth the Second eyes left men…

(*Eyes left; hold breath.*) …at ease.

*All breathe, burst with laughter. They inhale.*

Lime trees. We swim around Aphrodite's Rock…

*Sound: water, splashing. Light: spot on MOTHER, isolated.*

…anti-clockwise because it's a magic rock that gives you babies. We all swim…

*MOTHER does not move.*

…then splash in the waterfall that keeps you forever young like ancient Oil of Olay. An old man wants us to buy oranges.

*FATHER gives money. He looks proudly to CATHERINE as she calls to old man.*

Eff-Harry-Stow! (*To audience.*) Thank you is essential all over the world. The language is unimportant. The way you hold your head and your eyes means exactly what it means. You can't go wrong with a thank you. Eff-Harry-Stow.

*MEG and CATHERINE sneak away. FATHER panics.*

We're only looking for the waterfall again and…aah… look at the goats Meg! Aah!

*MEG and CATHERINE jerk.*

*During CATHERINE's narration, the family conveys changing dynamics: FATHER raises hand to MOTHER who, consumed by grief for baby, accepts threat of violence towards her and is oblivious to threat to girls. MEG watches FATHER, making him ashamed of his actions and speech. Adult CATHERINE observes the action as though for first time.*

(*As FATHER.*) Never wander off your mother has enough to deal with losing the baby selfish little bitches.

(*As MOTHER, wearily.*) No Clem don't tell them don't tell the girls.

(*As FATHER.*) Shut your mouth I'm the one working all the hours the one who gave up all this the one giving you class while I have to know what to damn well do don't look at me as though I've failed I'm not the one who carried on dancing smoking I'm not the stupid bitch who couldn't hang on to a foetus.

I didn't know about a nearly-baby. (*As adult, to MOTHER.*) *I* make father's first temper, it's *my* fault, but why don't you stand in front of Meg and me? Wrap around us?

(*As young self, to FATHER.*) It is my entire fault, father. We wanted to find that magic water to take home so that… (*Desperately finding a reason.*) we'll have anti-clockwise babies so we'll all be forever on holiday –

*FATHER sinks to knees; hugs MEG, who is afraid but defiant.*

(*As young self, to FATHER.*) Eff-Harry-Stow. (*To audience.*) I use it to this day. Can't go wrong with a thank you. Though I don't usually say it in Greek.

*Blackout.*

# Scene 14

*Same day, 3:40 pm. Hallway, Pontellier Avenue.*

*CATHERINE adds to wipe-board: 'Eff-Harry-Stow'. Walks up to Bedroom One. Looks fearfully into keyhole, then at agent's blurb.*

CATHERINE: Doesn't say Catherine's Room. It is my
room even after Cyprus, after the end of Enid Blyton life
and the start of a two-year concatenation of fatefulnesses.
(*Enters Bedroom One.*)

(*On tiptoes, overbalancing.*) You can just see the sea, a bluey
corner with the cliff in front like a bluey hanky sticking
out of a pocket. (*Looks down to garden. Becomes fearful.
Needs to exit but has nowhere to go.*)

(*Rubbing head.*) Going coming coming going. My
timetable lives a straight life and pulls me along its days
but today…

After the nearly-baby we impersonate a family. BaBa
BaBa BaBa BaBa Ba-Ba-Ba, BaBa BaBa BaBa BaBaaaaAA!
Even at the pictures.

*CATHERINE observes and joins in with the action from
downstage as family mime interaction with her young self.*

*Upstage: 1990: FATHER, MOTHER, MEG and (imagined)
CATHERINE at cinema. MOTHER fiddles nervously with
sweet wrapper. MEG and CATHERINE crunch sweets and
giggle. They mouth 'Pearl & Dean' theme. FATHER passes
threat along the row.*

(*Facing front.*) What? What was so bad about just being
happy to be on the earth? I still go every Tuesday.
Classic Movies From The Golden Age. It's easier when
you only have black and white to deal with. But this
week I watched a film straight through twice, waiting for
a different ending.

(*Anxious whisper.*) Usually he comes from behind. To
catch us, case we're laughing, at him. Don't know why he
thinks that. He's not a funny person.

*Blackout.*

# Scene 15

*Five days earlier: Wednesday, 2 pm. Flashback Area: Proscenium arch Theatre.*

CATHERINE: Every Wednesday pm I go to the theatre in a minibus with The Friends. (*Sits facing upstage. She copies clapping. Turns.*)

Where is the string, the itness that pulls people into one person like a ruched curtain? That makes a theatre hum when a cowboy sings happy to be on the American earth? That makes no one think it strange to be in a field with an imperceptible orchestra?

(*Waving madly.*) Deaf people don't clap, they wave. To say thank you. You have to be careful doing a deaf wave. (*Stops.*) You could be telling dirty jokes and not know it.

Last Wednesday: an old gentleman next to me (*As OLD GENTLEMAN.*) If you need to powder your nose I shall clear the row I shall shout fire isn't theatre exhilarating…

(*Turns downstage. Whispers.*) A man is on the type of grass you get in John Lewis's window. He is wearing tights and thinking. Word-pictures… (*Nodding in rhythm.*) I'm nearly in it, the world…through the eyes of an old blind gentleman.

*Blackout.*

# Scene 16

*1 May 2000. 3:50 pm. Master Bedroom, Pontellier Avenue.*

*Window is open. Sound: sea, distant.*

*CATHERINE notices FATHER's polished shoes on bed. Deflects. Reads blurb.*

CATHERINE: 'The master bedroom enjoys sea glimpses… (*Looks out then down to garden.*) and is situated over the kitchen and integral garage.' If you want to get to the garden you have to go past the kitchen, unless…

*Opens window; moves away; rushes at it; considers jumping to avoid kitchen/garage route. Her lips are forced by sea wind into rubber band-like smile.*

It isn't real smiling. You can stop a real smile. Unless you are at a funeral when someone blows off. You can stop if your father says you're doing a nasty smile even when you swear on brownie's honour. You can stop look away. Unless you are Meg.

(*Looks to garden. Becomes excited, childlike; sits on ledge.*) Father, chasing us, going (*Head back like a dog.*) ya-roooops! Swishing up the secret garden… I'm behind the wheelbarrow, Meg by the shed…he's coming… Ya-roooops!

*Sound – off: shrieks, giggling until breathless.*

Then Cyprus…these rooms get whispery…my mother gets… Meg is the last to look away from him, always.

*She looks to the door; loses balance; nearly falls out of window; recovers.*

Meg has an entirely brown body in summer with sticky curls like black blood down her face…the joy of it comes in my throat…even after Cyprus…mother me twelve Meg eleven our beach hut over there…and the day that becomes all days.

*Fade…to MEG 'la-lahing' etc. while CATHERINE gets into position…*

# Scene 17

*1991: Flashback Area: beach – that spills into the actual house.*

*Sound: sea, gulls, children playing.*

*CATHERINE interacts directly with MEG. MEG is ants-in-her-pants active.*

CATHERINE: Your legs are like humpy bridges.

MEG: Because I run.

CATHERINE: Hard and woody like skittles.

MEG: Because I run.

CATHERINE: You never stop running.

MEG: What is it mum says?

CATHERINE: (*Northern accent.*) You'll meet yourself coming back.

MEG: Because I run.

CATHERINE: Everywhere. Running is what you do.

MEG: And this… (*She dances, twists, 'la-lahs'.*) Ooh my back, quick I'm itching!

CATHERINE: You're sunburned.

MEG: I'm burning quick Cathy-Cath scratch between my shoulder-things. Oh I'm going to die I'm dying…

*CATHERINE scratches calmly. MEG leaps to rock pool; balances on her bottom.*

(*Pacy.*) Look Cathy-Cath pea crabs that's a razor shell that's a striped Venus that's a carpet shell that's a…bit of something this is a whatdoyoucallit ninety-nine shell…

*CATHERINE mouths 'common whelk'.*

…common whelk this one won't open come out thing-inside I won't laugh I promise pleeeease come out this one's a frothy wedding dress I'm never getting married I'm living with you and mum up there that house up the

cliff. (*Holding shells to eyes.*) Look shell-eyes shell-eyes!
Mum, look! Shell-eyes!

*MOTHER, in distance, smiles. MEG runs onto groyne.*

CATHERINE: Meg! We're not allowed on the groyne…
Meg!

MEG: Cathy-Cath! A cormorant, at the end, all caught up.
(*She inches forward; loses balance; shrieks.*)

CATHERINE: Meg, come back now.

MEG: Pumping its little wings…it's drowning it's dying –

CATHERINE: No, it can't drown. It's…a phoenix and
phoenixes can't drown, come back now, don't look
back…that's it…

*They run across beach; MEG lies face up in the sand, arms
by side.*

MEG: Bury me don't get sand in my willy-hole.

*CATHERINE starts to bury her.*

That house. We won't let anyone in. We'll never marry
he's a big lot of piss we'll die before he makes me cry
again before he makes me say sorry for every bloody-
fuck thing she's a liar saying she's just got bruisey blood,
that he's cruel to be kind –

CATHERINE: She's a silly laughy dancey-backwards mum
and lost the nearly-baby. We have to wait for father to
forgive her.

MEG: Don't leave me Cathy-Cath I'll drown you won't
leave me –

*CATHERINE strokes MEG's hair. MEG lies back.*

Itch my nose it's brilliant find that Welsh boy tell that
Sheena to join in tell mum you're burying me tell her it's
brilli –

*Enter FATHER. In one movement, he pulls MEG from the sand by her hair; she struggles. FATHER laughs; prompts them to join the 'game'. Light up on MOTHER, isolated, on deckchair. She stands, but only looks; smiles to the tourists. FATHER frogmarches MEG…off. MOTHER self-consciously follows…off. CATHERINE goes to her downstage position and watches with rising panic.*

CATHERINE: Meg, say sorry say it say thank you for keeping us from the tourist children so we don't catch delinquency say it Meg don't answer back play the game.

*Upstage: car. All face upstage. FATHER drives, MOTHER next to him, MEG and (imagined) CATHERINE in back. With one hand he removes (army) tie; flings it to MOTHER. We see his eyes in rear-view mirror. MOTHER looks at him. Without turning, she feels behind for MEG. As they touch, FATHER turns to MOTHER. She lets go of MEG.*

In the car Meg won't look away won't say it…she's not saying sorry not saying thank you… I'm sent to bed no dinner no kiss no drink (*As if seeing MOTHER for first time.*) say it mother say Catherine have a drink say Meg come inside say it mother, mum…

Meg is locked *in* the car not saying thank you mother's in the kitchen –

*FATHER stares at MEG.*

(*As FATHER.*) – *when* you apologise, *when* you show gratitude for my intervention at the beach *then* you may come inside.

*FATHER stares. MEG twists, 'lah-lah's' in her seat, never taking eyes from FATHER.*

…not putting her hand up not saying no. I'm in bed (*She is not.*) I don't see any more. (*Closes/opens eyes.*)

*FATHER turns away; freezes. MEG clambers into drivers'
seat; mimics FATHER's demeanour, staring in the mirror
manically hitting switches etc…*

*Lights down half to indicate passage of time…*

*Stops, looks down. Holds up glowing cigar lighter, then
FATHER's tie.*

*Lights down…up: the car is on fire.*

Meg drowning in fire pumping her little wings not
saying sorry thank you…but she knows I won't let her
drown I promised so she isn't trying hard enough to get
out doesn't think this could be her last entire day ever.

MEG: Cathy-Cath I'm burning I'm drowning…

*MOTHER moves towards the car; the flames are too high.
FATHER pulls her back. CATHERINE looks to FATHER,
to MOTHER. They are frozen.*

CATHERINE: (*Hoarsely.*) No! (*Helplessly, trying to open the
car door.*) No!

*Fade MEG/car.*

*CATHERINE goes downstage. Faces front.*

(*As POLICEMAN.*) Sir, don't blame yourself if a man
with your skills couldn't save your little girl no one
could that's a fact.

*Upstage: MOTHER shakes uncontrollably. FATHER cries;
goes downstage. Whispers to CATHERINE.*

(*As FATHER.*) That could have been you.

*CATHERINE is frozen; mouths 'Thank you'.*

*End of Act One.*

# ACT TWO

## Scene 1

*1 May 2000. 4 pm. Hallway, Pontellier Avenue.*

*CATHERINE sits on stairs, looking wide-eyed through the banisters.*

CATHERINE: (*Pacy, concentrating, monotone.*) There is a book called The Dictionary of Etymology. It shows you the beginnings of the beginning and end of a word so that you know why you are saying it. It is the root. If you asked for the book, you would make sure you said etymology not entomology. Or you would end up knowing why you are saying the beginning and end of insects.

*FATHER calmly walks up the stairs; as he passes CATHERINE, he steps on her skirt. She leaps down the stairs as FATHER enters Master Bedroom...to black.*

(*During next speech, she vigorously brushes skirt.*) Monday library Tuesday pictures Wednesday theatre Thursday The Safe Way Friday post office Saturday Community Centre Sunday launderette dry pants (*Walks in circles.*) Monday May Day 2000: Ward Seventeen Mr Mr and Mr Estate Agents Twenty-one Pontellier Avenue and words nearly coming...heart-thundery disobedient words...stinging, beating...septic cuts...today entirely twenty-one entirely don't have an operation should be having it now instead I'm meeting myself coming back Ward Sister Pam Island says I shouldn't be Bamboozled tells the doctor off she is magnificent – (*Stops. Reels. Grasps banister. Feels along it.*)

Meg's coffin makes a dent. The men have to reverse out of the dining room towards the...kitchen. (*Looks at blurb.*) The dent isn't on the list of things to tell the buyer. When I move to the Children's Home, this lady buys it.

Not put off by the papers. Meg's head: going up and down because the men can't drive an eleven year-old's body out of a door.

*Turns. FATHER, dressed for MEG's funeral, peers through the banister. CATHERINE shrieks; moves towards kitchen. She cannot go there. Goes to front door, yet she needs to complete this journey: now or never. Hits head until FATHER fades.*

One of the hymns is *The Lord is my Shepherd.* There are two tunes and I always sing the other one. I do it at Meg's funeral.

*Upstage: MOTHER and FATHER at funeral. He is obviously digging fingers into CATHERINE's shoulder for singing the wrong tune.*

(*Wincing.*) He has to choose things to remember since the nearly-baby and Meg's accident. Forgets that when I used to get the tune wrong – or the lady in front sang like a wobbly parrot – he used to smile into his hymn book. And my mother would start with her uncontrollable giggle. Sunday mornings were like that.

*Music: Michael Jackson's 'Dirty Diana'.*

*Upstage: Sunday morning, 1989. FATHER in bed. MEG enters: leaps on the bed like a water bomb. Enter MOTHER with tray. FATHER goes under bed for slippers; bashes head. All giggle. MOTHER hands out toast; leaves plate on FATHER's side. He sits on bed, on the toast. All burst with tears of laughter. MOTHER kisses FATHER. He returns the kiss, passionately. CATHERINE double-takes as she sees this sexual power for first time.*

*Fade upstage scene.*

(*Proudly, yet disturbed at new perception of past.*) My family. (*Goes to wipe-board. It is full with 'thank you' phrases.*)

A week before my mother and father die, I am accused of inflammatory libel. English essay. Subject: (*Writes.*) 'My Family.' (*Recites.*) 'My Family by Catherine Hope Swan. I lived with my sister, mother and father in Enid Blyton life until two years ago when my mother lost a nearly-baby, we went to Cyprus and came back not exactly My Family. My house got cleaner. Meg had boot polish on her tongue to teach her not to swear. Her death last May is a mystery to all. I do not like shouting and bruisey skin.'

Mrs Michaelson calls it (*As Mrs Michaelson.*) A tissue of fiction your father is an honourably-discharged British Army officer I shall tell him what an ungrateful girl...

Tissues of fiction. (*She lights up.*) But I know about a light part, an itness... I'm quick and sharp and join onto words without thinking, like a novel that means what it means. I just am. I'm the middle of my entire world learning a new thing every day full of words of promise of grade A's of bigthingness then my father kills my mother.

(*Waits for the sky to fall in. Goes to front door.*) Go back go back now.

(*Stops by wipe-board. Rubs out words.*) Where are mine? (*Rubs head furiously.*) So much all-the-time noise. Like the Major Fford-Trenchant Home For Children and Young Adults. The town knows us as Majorettes. A Home for normal people. I am normal. I just have entirely hurting hips and dead parents.

(*As Children.*) (*1.*) Why don't you live with your parents (*2.*) why do you walk like a penguin (*3.*) do you like my pencil case my mummy sent it from prison how much sex have you done (*4.*) can't you talk what's the matter with your talk box?

So all-the-time loud. Until I'm eighteen and leave and have to do my own timetable.

In The Waltons, when Jim-Bob, Jason, Mary-Ellen, Elizabeth, Ben, John-Boy or Erin leaves home or Mrs Walton goes to have her TB seen to, they get the bus from Mr Godsey's store. The entire family waves them off. Forty-five minutes later the entire family is on the porch waving them back and the returning person says you sure appreciate the mountain and daddy's sawmill and mama's cornbread. Then they say goodnight in every possible combination like they are doing country dancing. They never do any sex. I didn't don't haven't not since my father died.

*Bedroom One: flash of FATHER, taking off shirt.*

(*An involuntary memory. She calls weakly.*) Mum...mum.

*MOTHER stands just out of reach.*

(*To MOTHER.*) Let's come home. You there Meg here...write it write 'My Family'...

*MOTHER walks to kitchen to black. CATHERINE is frozen.*

No one to check the heels of my socks. No one to run away from bits of crab with. No one to teach me to dance backwards or pat my shoulder when I say Eff-Harry-Stow.

Never no more salute the Queen's road or have a funeral for a hamster, be one-fourth of one whole. No pink birthdays or winks from the front row when I forget how to make the recorder do E flat. No help with plaits, choosing a bra. No one to tell about the new friend, new word. No one to tell myself to, who has a bit of myself inside them. In the entire world, no one. Sometimes I could howl like a baby dog. (*Weary with fear; tries to scream; nothing. Takes step towards kitchen. Hits head.*)

Sometimes you have to make a hole in the pie for the steam to escape or else your brain will cook itself dry. And you will go entirely mad.

(*Takes step closer.*) I stop going to the world at thirteen.

(*Step closer. Stops.*) You can just stop. Stop your world stop being in it stop being. Stop.

(*Knows she must move today. Towards kitchen…*) BaBa BaBa BaBa BaBa Ba-Ba-Ba…buy two get one free buy… BaBa BaBa BaBa BaBaaaaAA…thank you.

(*Stops outside kitchen; holds aching stomach.*) The root of 'menorraghia' means month rage. It is medical to do with being female and knowing it every month. Now I'm now showing you ten am today Ward Seventeen Dorset South Hospital…

# Scene 2

*Same day, 10 am. Flashback Area: Ward 17, Dorset South Hospital.*

CATHERINE: (*As STUDENT NURSE.*) I'm going to rattle through you I'm late for my break. Hop on the scales. Confirm you have no pacemaker nicotine patch contact lenses false teeth false legs shrapnel irregular bowels asthma diabetes alcoholism allergies epilepsy. Are you: blind deaf vegan psychotic pregnant Catholic HIV positive not a native English speaker? Your surgery is a consequence of menorraghia. Some medical ethics law says sign here if you're happy. If you sit on the bed take your shoes off this isn't a doss-house here's a booklet I need a Kit-Kat.

(*Watches her go. Mouths 'thank you'. Tugs at a plastic ID bracelet.*) In case I get myself mixed up with someone else. Or the doctor does and tries to cut out my liver.

I've brought everything on the list but except a dressing-gown. I should have known it was open-plan: I watch *Holby City*. The actors usually have a railing sticking out of their blouse. Under those conditions you would forget your dressing-gown.

*Looks opposite; nods in reaction to another patient – Doreen, Scottish.*

(*As Doreen.*) I'm Doreen you pay fifty years for the NHS they couldn't give a monkey's tits if you're terminal I only came for a scrape you'd think I was asking for the moon God knows what you've got under that dish the one before was one of them Asians there's only us two here yet they won't answer the bell. You could be dying.

There *isn't* only us two. In the corner, facing the window. Old lady.

(*Picks up booklet.*) I'm having this: Sub-total Hysterectomy and Bilateral Salpingo-Oopherectomy.

(*Lies back on bed; lifts arm; lets it fall.*) Everything is done for you, to you. You don't lift a hand. You lie in a bed and only worry about not having a dressing-gown, and the time taken off your hand. (*She sinks lower down the bed, in surrender to having nothing.*)

*Sound: distant TV.*

'Early Morning With Mal and Minty'…phone-in. Post-traumatic stress. Ingrid, Ashton-under-Lyne… (*As Ingrid.*) ever since I saw footage of a fire on the London Underground I can't go under the stairs for the Hoover… (*As MINTY.*) treat yourself, Ingrid, have your roots done – Mal? (*As MAL.*) pull yourself together Ingrid sue the BBC for showing the news… (*As INGRID.*) Thanks, Mal, I love your show.

(*CATHERINE is suddenly aware of someone. Reads name badge.*) Ward Sister Pam Island. (*Slides down the bed; the rubber mattress makes a noise.*)

It was the bed. Ward Sister Pam Island is leaving my sheet open like the sign on a plague house. Thinking it was me blowing off.

(*Suddenly, her legs are lifted and put down.*) A pillow under my knees. Ward Sister Pam knows about my hips!

(*Tries to say thank you.*) The words voice clear part...gone I'm afraid.

(*Lifts arm. Doesn't let it fall.*) Afraid! Afraid of feeling comfortable and nothing, afraid of tomorrow, an operation I should not have. Afraid of my voice and my light part being swallowed like gulpy tomatoes entirely forever, of the time already taken. I am afraid. It is what I am.

*Touches throat; tries to push the words. Her hand is held, patted. About to speak –*

*Sound: bell; flashing light.*

*CATHERINE watches PAM go to light. Pats own hand; puts it against her cheek.*

(*As PAM.*) I know my love I know.

*Stands; watches staff around old lady's bed; rising panic.*

*Sound: bells, buzzers, louder...long beep as old lady dies.*

(*She pulls back sheet; there is no old lady.*) Me! It is entirely me!

(*Scrabbles among sheets; becomes less articulate.*) Afraid of...flat-house...timetable... Afraid of those things: Ward Seventeen, empty visitor's chair – and the future of those things: the long beep. You *should* be afraid! You should feel being afraid then not let it *be* you, do its fear to you. You should not be done to. You should do. I see it...so can a navy blurry someone. Ward Sister Pam – (*She slumps to floor.*)

*Blackout.*

# Scene 3

*Same day, 4:15 pm. Outside kitchen, Pontellier Avenue.*

*CATHERINE holds aching stomach.*

*During speech, she rushes through rooms – except kitchen – looking for MOTHER.*

*Meanwhile, we see MOTHER in Master Bedroom, dressed in black coat for MEG's funeral. She finishes polishing FATHER's shoes. Distracted by a noise, she leaves them on the bed. While CATHERINE is in lounge, MOTHER rushes down the stairs; feels newly-made dent in banister. Silently agonised, she goes into kitchen…to black.*

CATHERINE: Doreen says (*As Doreen.*) You're getting off lightly I don't know if I'm having a scrape or a post-mortem.

Ward Sister Pam tells the surgeon I shouldn't have an operation when I don't have anyone to shout no. (*As PAM.*) People Like Her Are Always Bamboozled. The surgeon calls me a subnormal bed-waster.

*CATHERINE sees MOTHER disappear into kitchen; compelled to follow.*

Viewers will find the kitchen self-explanatory.

# Scene 4

*CATHERINE's thirteenth birthday, 1 May 1992. Kitchen, Pontellier Avenue.*

*She interacts directly with MOTHER; helps her to bake cake. MOTHER wears apron.*

*Sound: Michael Jackson's 'Off the Wall'.*

*MOTHER adds 13 to cake; puts cream on CATHERINE's nose. They laugh, but look to door. They relax; MOTHER uses spoon as mic; dances backwards; mimics Jackson.*

*Sound: music up.*

CATHERINE: (*Joining in.*) Look at me mum, I'm doing this!

*MOTHER adds candle; they clap, sing, dance, laugh. Enter FATHER, unseen by them. He turns up the music. CATHERINE and MOTHER freeze.*

*Blackout.*

*We hear loud exhalation from MOTHER.*

(*To FATHER, hurriedly, placatory.*) Thank you thank you thank you –

*End of Act Two.*

# ACT THREE

## Scene 1

*1 May 2000. 4:30 pm. Kitchen, Pontellier Avenue.*

*Lights: spot on adult CATHERINE, frozen. Sound: her heavy breathing…louder. Cut.*

*Past and present moments are compressed into this one. CATHERINE is marooned.*

*Lights: spot on FATHER looking in through back door. He is contrite, ruined. Yet, he is blocking CATHERINE's exit.*

*CATHERINE tries to remove him by looking as defiant and accusing as MEG would. She looks all directions for an escape route…*

*Lights: spot on MOTHER in centre of kitchen. She puts out a hand to CATHERINE, who pulls away nearer back door.*

MOTHER: You'll meet yourself coming back!

> *CATHERINE faces front. MOTHER stands behind and puts arm around CATHERINE. CATHERINE resists. MOTHER holds the arm tight then the other until CATHERINE is enveloped, but still faces front. FATHER steps into kitchen.*
>
> *CATHERINE is rigid but does not try to escape MOTHER's longed-for strength.*
>
> *Lights: spot on MEG, balancing as though on beach groyne.*

CATHERINE: Phoenixes can't drown, Meg. I made that up.

MEG: (*Giggling.*) Look Mum – shell-eyes, shell-eyes! Cathy, Cathy-Cath! Father, dad…daddy – shell-eyes!

> *Lights: spots on FATHER, MOTHER and CATHERINE – entranced by MEG/life. Fade MEG.*

*CATHERINE – still held – turns in one movement into MOTHER. Inhales perfume; becomes distressed. MOTHER walks her – still enveloped – past FATHER to back door.*

*MOTHER opens arms as CATHERINE gathers momentum and can carry on alone…*

*Fade to black.*

*End of Act Three.*

# ACT FOUR

## Scene 1

*1 May 2000. 6 pm. Altar, church opposite CATHERINE's flat.*

CATHERINE: (*Calm, matter-of-fact.*) That is why my hips hurt. They hurt because my father jumps on my pelvis, both feet on it. Making it the last second I'm joined to my spleen and right ovary. Then he does the same to my head and spills my words across the tiles. If we lived in olden times, you would call me a cripple. He makes it look easy, doesn't he, a rolling pin breaking biscuits.

(*Drops to knees; faces altar; clasps hands, closes eyes; speaks in rhythm of prayer.*) I'm waiting
for you mother
to get my father off
do what you never did for Meg
get my father off be my mother shout no
but you tried to be a mother to my father too
I forgive you as
forever and ever mother you drown
in cake and blood amen.

*Silence.*

This is the church opposite my flat-house with its matching community centre. (*Looking around.*) There is a lady on television called Carol Smiling who tells people their rooms are horrible then does a laugh that makes your ears itch. She would stencil the organ and spray the Virgin Hot Pink.

(*A trolley with candles; she puts three coins in a box; puts three candles in a row.*) It's only sixty pence for your entire family. (*She lights candles. Walks downstage.*)

*Behind her: lights: sister candle glows. Sound: musical birthday candle.*

*CATHERINE is startled but – with awareness of MEG's spirit and her own potential power – she carries on walking…*

*Fade to black.*

# Scene 2

*Same day, 6:15 pm. Bench outside church as night falls.*

*CATHERINE sits at one end.*

CATHERINE: I've done so much today I'm meeting myself coming back. It is still Monday May Day. Last time I came was to a Princess Diana service. Everyone ran in with their roses. I copied – only I can't run unless I want to look like Douglas Bader fleeing the Germans. You queued down the aisle then wrote then dabbed your eyes. The one before me put 'Paparazzi Scum Rot In Hell P.S. Same To Prince Charles'. I was grateful to sit – Princess Diana had stopped my hips hurting! So I wrote 'thank you'.

(*Stands; shifts weight.*) You feel guilty feeling pain when some people are dead and can't feel a thing. Eight years I've been on the edge of death, putting my key into the door of it, wanting it, deserving it, then today…hiss-puck. Not even pop like a shooty cork, but hiss-puck, a gone-off bottle of champagne.

That is it, the ends of fear. You can't go further than that.

*Sound: sea, distant.*

The beach hut washed away. The sand isn't the same sand – comes from Africa in ships and runs straight to the beach like it's on holiday.

*Sound: piano music from community centre; chaotic tap-dancing; teacher: 'shu-ffle hop-step shu-ffle-ball-change…' etc.*

(*Moves feet, still sitting; begins to pull it all together. Pacy.*)
You give a word to someone…they make it new like a
ball-change…you speak shu-ffle ball-change…things
*happen.* You feel a new word looping your tongue, you
see a play press Enter pat someone's hand…you say yes!
I've nearly got it! Nearly got what you've got: the itness!
I'm just like you, just about attached to the bones of the
world.

*Sound: tap-dancing becomes syncopated.*

(*CATHERINE joins in, still seated; covers smile.*) On a
bench in the dark in a graveyard, tap-dancing. This is
living.

(*The absurdity hits her; becomes more urgent, animated,
tapping. Stands.*) Today is my twenty-first birthday, my
father was forty-three when he died, every day is Father's
Day and Mother's Day and I'm sick of it, if this is living.
My father was me and my mother was me and my sister
was me because that is what I was born into. But for
ninety-six months it's me (*Taps.*) me (*Taps.*) me (*Taps.*)
with hurting hips and Ba-Ba-Ba's me me me and I'm sick
of it.

(*Stops, breathless.*) This is me. And what I can do now I'm
leaving my head.

(*Sits near middle of bench, exhausted.*) I've done so much
today I'm meeting myself.

I don't want to live this timetable of heart-hurt every
twenty-four hours, this story. At least a novel ends. I am
not a novel – least, not a classical one because I get
my Greeks and Romans inter-mixed. I can't invent a
millennial philosophy or write the state of the nation.
I can't be those big thingnesses.

'Normal' is about small things: reading between other *humans* lines then seeing a bit of yourself. I hope you can see it is not a no-thing, that I am not a no-thing, that I am a thing at least.

No sound, but moving words, to our world. With me in it.

(*Sits dead centre. Opens mouth; stops. Opens mouth wide. Stops.*) Look at me mum, I'm doing this.

*Sits still, silent, in her own centre. Tentatively smiles...into a broad fearless grin.*

*Upstage: MOTHER, behind bench, does same smile and mouths 'Thank You'.*

*Sound: musical candle playing 'Happy Birthday'...*

*Fade to black... Play-out music: Michael Jackson's 'Off The Wall'.*

*The End.*